IGOR STRAVII

SUITE FROM

L'OISEAU DE FEU

(Reorchestrated by the composer, 1919)

for

ORCHESTRA

FULL SCORE

Material available on hire

CHESTER MUSIC

ORCHESTRE

2 flûtes, 2 hautbois et cor anglais, 2 clarinettes
2 bassons, 4 cors en Fa, 2 trompettes en Ut,
3 trombones, tuba, timballes, grosse caisse,
piatti, triangle, xylophon, harpe, pianoforte,
2 violons, alto, cello, contre-basse.

Suite de L'OISEAU DE FEU

RÉORCHESTRÉE PAR L'AUTEUR EN 1919

IGOR STRAWINSKY

Introduction

M.M. ♩ = 108

GRAN CASSA

VIOLE

VIOLONCELLI

CONTRABASSI

Tr.ni

Gr.C.

Viole

V.lli

C.B.

Cl.in La

Fag.

Corni in Fa

Tr.in Do

Tr.ni

Gr.C.

Arpa

V.ni II.

Viole

V.lli

C.B.

L'oiseau de feu et sa danse

Variation de l'oiseau de feu

Ronde des princesses

KHOROVODE

24

Danse infernale du roi Kastcheï

12
Fl. picc.
Fl.gr.
Ob.
Cl.
Fag.
Corni
Tr.be
I. II.
Tr.ni
III.
Tuba
Timp.
Gr. C.
Piano.
Arpa.
V.ni I.
V.ni II.
Viole
V.lli
C. B.
sfff
mf
f
pp
pp sub.

30

6
II.
Fl.
mf
Oboe
I. mf
Cl.
I.
Corni
Piano
f
f sim.
mp
sons etouffés
Arpa
sim.
Vni I.
jeté
Vni II.
f
Viole
Vlli
jeté f
arco
C.B.
pizz.
*CUT TO FIG 21
7
Fl.
Oboi
Cl.
Fag.
Corni.
sempre poco sf
Piano
Arpa
Vni I.
Vni II.
Viole
Vlli
C.B.
f

11
Fl. picc.
Fl. gr.
Oboi
Cl.
Fag.
Corni
Tr.be
Tr.ni
Tuba
Timp.
Xiloph.
Piano
Arpa
V.ni I.
V.ni II.
Viole
V.lli
C.B.
sf
ff
mf
très sec.
a 2
I. bouché-cuivré
poco sf
I.
II. III.
II.
III.
I. II. a 2
baguettes en bois
f
sff non arpegg.
non arpegg.
sff
arco unis.
sff très sec
arco

44

123

19

Fl. picc.

Fl. gr.

Oboi

Cl.

Fag.

Corni

Tr.be

Tr.ni

Tuba

Timp.

Piano

glissando des
touches blanches
m.d.

Arpa

19

V.ni I.

V.ni II.

Viole

V.lli

C. B.

pizz.

20
Fl. picc.
Fl. gr.
Oboi
Cl.
Fag.
Corni
sim.
Tr. be
Tr. ni
Tuba
Timp.
Piano
Arpa
do♭
V. ni I.
V. ni II.
Viole
V. lli
C. B.

138
Fl. picc.
Fl. gr.
Oboi
Cl.
Fag.
Corni
Tr.be
Tr.ni
sim.
Tuba
Timp.
f
f
Piano
Arpa
V.ni I.
V.ni II.
Viole
V.lli
C. B.

48

157
23
Fl. picc.
Fl. gr.
Oboi
a 2
ff
Cl.
Corni
Sola
con sord.
fff
Tr.be
I.
II.
f
ff marcatiss.
Tr.ni
Tr.ne III
Tuba
Piano
Arpa
div.
arco
V.ni I.
V.ni II.
Viole
V.lli
C. B.

170

25
Fl. picc.
sff
sff sempre
ff
Fl. gr.
Oboi
I.
II.
ff
Cl.
I.
II.
ff
Fag.
I.
II.
f staccatissimo (très sec.)
Corni
II.
I. II.
III. IV.
ff
Tr.be
I. II.
ff très court
Tr.ni
I. II.
ff très court
Xyloph.
sf
sf
8
Piano
sff
simile
ff
Arpa
ff
25
V.ni I.
ff
V.ni II.
ff
ff
Viole
ff
V.lli
mp
ff
C. B.
pizz.
f

55

28   29 Più mosso (♩.)

Fl.picc.

Fl.gr.

Oboi

Cl.

Fag.   *sempre ff*

Corni

Tr.be   *sempre f*

Tr.ni   *simile*

Tr.ni e
Tuba

Tamb. de   avec le pouce
B.que

Triang.

Piatti

Gr.C.

Piano

28   29 Più mosso (♩.)
                           pizz.
V.ni I.

V.ni II.   pizz.

Viole   unis. tutte   pizz.
         arco
V.lli   unis. tutti   pizz.
         arco
C.B.   unis. tutti
         arco

30
Oboi
I.II.
Fag.
I. II.
Corni
I.II.
III. IV.
sempre sim.
sff
Tr.be
I.
II.
Tr.ni
I.
II.
Tr.ni e Tuba
III.
Timp.
Changez le La en Mi grave
f
Gr.C.
Piano
30
V.ni I.
arco
sff
pizz.
f
arco
très fort
V.ni II.
div.
div.
arco
pizz.
f
arco
très fort
Viole
arco
non div.
pizz.
f
sff
arco
très fort
V.lli
arco
pizz.
sff
f
arco
très fort
C.B.
sff

58

(*) Le DO grave = pour les C.B. qui en possedent.

63

Berceuse

Final

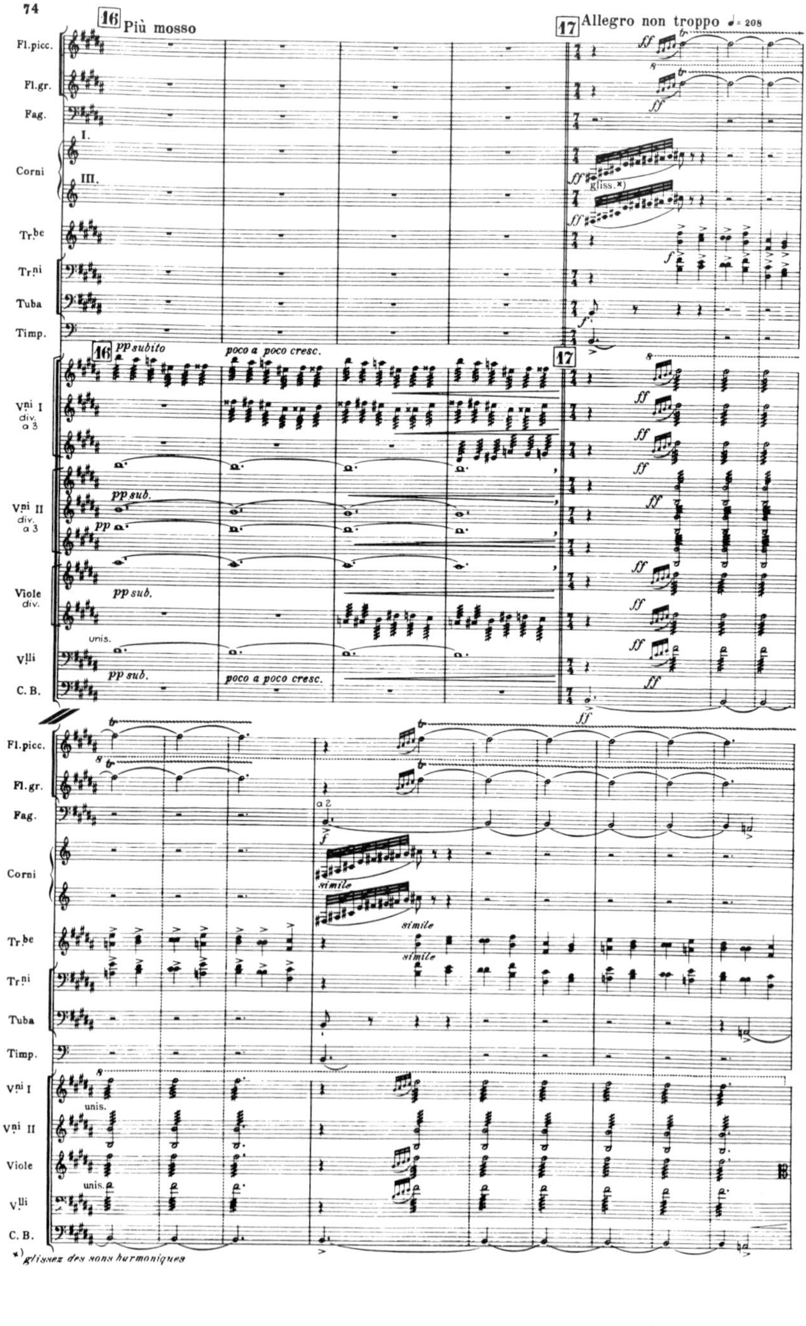

*) glissez des sons harmoniques

78